THE NATURE COMPANY

# SCALY & SLIMY

## In 3-D!

**Photographs by David G. Burder**
**Text by Rick and Susan Sammon**

**Starrhill Press**
**Washington, D.C.**

# Scaly, Slimy, and Lovable

The scaly and slimy animals in this book might seem scary. In truth, very few of the millions of scaly and slimy creatures on earth can hurt you—and even these types won't unless injured or afraid.

Like all animals, scalies and slimies need our protection to survive in an ever-changing environment. For example, snakes are often killed by frightened people. But most snakes are harmless, and they play an important role in the ecosystem. They eat pests like mice and rats. In turn, birds such as owls, eagles, and hawks feed on snakes.

Even lizards terrify some people. Instead we should be grateful to these reptiles for keeping the insect population in check. Just imagine what it would be like if there were lots more stinging and biting and buzzing insects outside—or inside! Lizards, like all living things on our planet, are important to the balance of nature. The removal of just one species from an area can upset the balance.

Habitat destruction is another reason slimy and scaly

creatures—and many of the world's animals—are in danger. When rain forests are cut down or wetlands drained, many living things are killed. The ones that escape lose their homes and may eventually die. Again, imagine what it would be like without the "jug-a-rum" call of a bull frog around a pond, or the "peep, peep" of a tree frog on a warm summer night.

Don't get us wrong—we know it's fun to hold a frog or turtle by a stream, find a salamander under a rock, or observe a snake slithering through grass. It's even more thrilling if you know something about the animals. But please remember not to harm these critters or disturb their habitats.

Scaly and slimy creatures were here on earth long before humans. It's a small planet, and all species, including people, plants, and animals, must share the space to ensure our mutual survival.

**Rick and Susan Sammon**

*Croton-on-Hudson, New York*

BOAS and pythons, like all snakes, are reptiles. They are fierce hunters. The boa constrictor, pictured here, uses the scaly, powerful coils of its body to strangle or crush its prey. Then the snake swallows and digests the animal in one piece. If the victim is as large as a deer, finishing the meal might take a few hours. After such a big dinner, the boa wouldn't need to eat for a month.

### DEFENSES

A boa will "play dead" by lying motionless on the ground to fool predators. This ploy works because many predators will not eat a dead animal. A boa can also puff out its body so it seems even bigger and scarier than usual.

### FUN FACT

It is difficult for a boa to see in the dark. Still the snake is able to hunt at night. Through a special nerve in an opening on the top of its head, the boa detects the body heat of birds and mammals to go after and grab.

### SCIENCE EXTRA

Boas give birth to live young, which break out of thin shells as the eggs are laid.

# LIZARDS

LIZARDS come in a rainbow of colors that help conceal them from predators and prey. This bearded dragon is very hard to see when it rests on rocks. A chameleon can change from one color to another to another, so it can blend in with lots of different hiding places.

### PHYSICAL CHARACTERISTICS
The bearded dragon can run very fast on its four legs. Some types of lizards have only two legs and some have none at all. A legless lizard moves by slithering like a snake.

### HABITAT
Most types of lizards are found in warm climates like the desert or the tropical rain forest. Still, it's possible to find several species of lizard in cold places not far from the North Pole.

### SCIENCE EXTRA
When a bird or another predator attacks a lizard, sometimes the lizard's tail breaks off. If the lizard escapes to safety it will grow a new tail.

### FUN FACT
The word "dinosaur" means terrible lizard. Can you see the resemblance?

GECKOS, unlike most lizards, have "voices." At night the male sings "geck oh, geck oh," probably to communicate with friends and mates. This leopard gecko, also called the panther gecko, grows to be about 12 inches long.

 **PHYSICAL CHARACTERISTICS**
A gecko has special toes that let it crawl up walls and even upside-down across ceilings.

 **HABITAT**
In the wild, leopard geckos feed on grasshoppers, scorpions, beetles, and spiders. In some places geckos are welcome pets, because they will eat household pests, like spiders, mosquitoes, and even cockroaches.

 **SCIENCE EXTRA**
The leopard gecko has movable eyelids. Most other species of gecko have eyes that are permanently covered with a transparent lid. Many geckos have freaky looking eyes because their pupils are vertical instead of round like other animals.

 **FUN FACT**
After eating, a gecko uses its long tongue to wipe off its face—including its eyeballs.

# TURTLES, like other reptiles, are cold blooded.

Reptiles need the sun to keep their body temperature correct. When it gets cold, this painted turtle warms up by resting in the sun or on warm rocks.

## PHYSICAL CHARACTERISTICS
A turtle's shell is made of horny scales and bone. Underneath, the turtle's skeleton is attached directly to the shell.

## PREY
Turtles have no teeth, but their sharp beaks can snap off plants and grab small insects, fish, and worms.

## HABITAT
The turtle lives in and near water but buries its eggs in a pit on land. When a baby turtle hatches it must claw its way up through the sand or dirt to the surface to take its first breath.

## SCIENCE EXTRA
After a baby turtle crawls up to the air, it must find its way to the water. For sea turtles, this distance can be as long as a football field. But if the turtle survives this first difficult journey, it might have quite a life ahead. Some types of sea turtles live to be 150 years old. That is an animal record!

SLUGS look like snails without shells. This garden slug excretes a slimy film and glides over it. The slime allows the slug to stick to walls, windows, and even ceilings. You can find a slug by following its slimy trail.

### HABITAT
During the day a garden slug hides under rocks, logs, and leaves. At night it comes out to eat fruit and vegetables. This diet makes farmers and gardeners consider slugs pests.

### PREDATORS
Slugs might look disgusting, but many other animals think they are tasty. In French restaurants, you can find the slug's cousin, the snail, on the menu.

### DEFENSE
To protect themselves from predators, slugs can shrink into tiny blobs that are difficult to see.

### SCIENCE EXTRA
A slug is neither a reptile nor an amphibian. It is a member of an animal group called the gastropods. You may think that all slugs look alike. In fact, there are more than 40 different kinds of these slimy creatures in the United States.

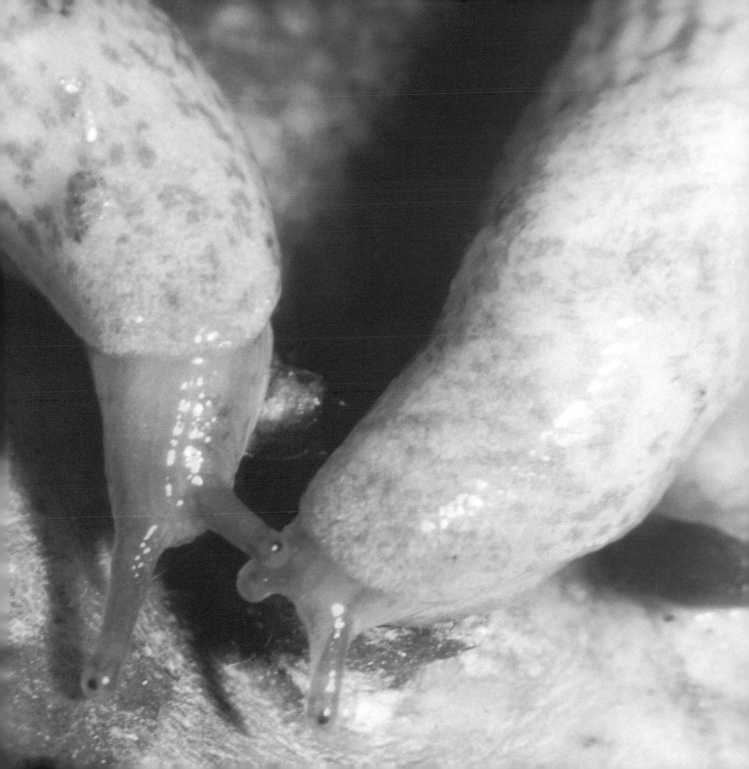

# FROGS

FROGS are amphibians, and so can live both on land and in water. The word "amphibian" means double life. While on land a frog breathes through its lungs. Under water, a frog breathes through its skin.

### HABITAT
This horned frog, like many frog species, lives near water in marshes and in woods. In the winter it digs a hole in the mud at the bottom of a pond or stream and sleeps. In the spring the horned frog wakes up and starts looking for a mate.

### PREY
With a quick flick of its sticky tongue, the frog swipes its meal off plants and rocks. A frog's tongue is so fast it can catch flying insects. This horned frog also eats small animals, including other frogs!

### FUN FACT
A frog needs wet skin to breathe. Over time a frog's skin dries out. The frog then grows a new moist skin as it sheds (and eats!) its old one.

### SCIENCE EXTRA
The largest frog in the world, the Goliath frog, lives in Africa, and it is as big as a football. The American tree frog is one of the smallest, and it is as small as your thumbnail.

# TREE FROGS

have very sticky pads on their super-long fingers and toes that help them climb trees, bushes, and tall grass. White's tree frog, in this picture, lives in Australia. Like the gecko, it is often kept as a pet in the bathroom and kitchen, where it eats pesky insects.

### PHYSICAL CHARACTERISTIC

White's tree frog grows to a length of only four inches. Still, it is considered a giant because it is four times as big as most other tree frogs.

### FUN FACT

Another species of Australian tree frog, the green and gold bell frog, lives mainly on reeds in the water instead of trees. When the male calls for its mate, it sounds like a saw cutting through wood.

### SCIENCE EXTRA

Frogs and toads are both part of the amphibious frog family. Frogs usually have wet, smooth skin while toad skin is dry, rough, and covered with warts. Toads have shorter legs than frogs and move more slowly, both in water and on land. A toad walks on land while a frog hops.

# SALAMANDERS

are amphibians. This tiger salamander can grow to be 15 inches long. It is the largest of all land-living salamanders. The biggest salamanders on earth live in Asia and reach lengths up to five feet.

 **PHYSICAL CHARACTERISTICS**
Tiger salamanders spend most of their time living under ground or beneath rocks. Female and males usually look alike, though the male's tail is longer.

 **PREY**
Soon after the sun goes down, the tiger salamander leaves its hiding place and begins to search for crickets, locusts, worms, mice, and small amphibians to eat.

 **HABITAT**
The tiger salamander will borrow the burrows of crayfish, mice, or rats for hiding places. Like many amphibians, adult salamanders live on land, but return to water to breed.

 **SCIENCE EXTRA**
When a salamander larvae hatches from the egg, it remains in the water. As it grows up and moves onto land, it loses its gills, and its flattened swimming tail becomes rounded.

# SCORPIONS

are feared because of the poisonous stingers in their tails. A scorpion will not attack a human, but will sting if stepped on or threatened. In some tropical and desert areas, a scorpion sting can be fatal. In these places people check their shoes where a scorpion might be hiding before putting them on to avoid being stung.

### PREY
The black scorpion, pictured here, eats crickets, spiders, centipedes, and millipedes. A scorpion also preys on other scorpions. In fact, the female may eat the male after mating.

### PREDATORS
The desert road runner and other birds hunt scorpions. Before eating, the bird bites off the bug's dangerous tail.

### FUN FACT
A scorpion carries her babies, which look like mini-versions of the mother, around on her back for about a month after birth.

### SCIENCE EXTRA
Do you think this scorpion looks like a lobster? Like a lobster, the bug has an exoskeleton, which means its skeleton is on the outside of its body.

SKINKS are a type of lizard. There are hundreds and hundreds of different species of skink. Most types range in size from 3 to 13 inches, but this one, the western blue-tongued skink, is a giant. It reaches a length of almost 18 inches.

### PHYSICAL CHARACTERISTICS

The blue-tongued skink is easily recognizable as a lizard, but many skinks look more like snakes with tiny feet and smooth skin. Some skinks have no feet at all.

### HABITAT

Many types of skinks, including the blue-tongued, live in Australia. Skinks are found on every continent except Antarctica.

### PREY

Most skinks feed on bugs and other tiny animals. Giant skinks, like the blue-tongued, also eat grasses and berries.

### SCIENCE EXTRA

Many types of skink lay eggs, but the blue-tongued gives birth to live young. When it is born, each baby skink is already half the size of its mother.

# IGUANAS are lizards. The male iguana is often much more colorful than the female. The male uses its flashy looks to attract a mate.

### PHYSICAL CHARACTERISTICS

The green iguana, shown here, can reach a length of five feet from the tip of its nose to the end of its tail. Its tail might be up to three times as long as its body. The animal uses its tail for slapping, to defend itself against predators such as snakes and birds.

### PREY

Iguanas look fierce, but most species eat only insects and small animals like snails.

### SCIENCE EXTRA

A mother iguana lays her eggs under a rock and leaves them. When the baby iguanas hatch, their instincts help them survive on their own.

### FUN FACT

The only marine iguana in the world lives in the Galapagos Islands in the Pacific Ocean. This lizard eats algae that grows under water on rocks.

PYTHONS and boas have neither fangs nor venom, but they do have sharp teeth. The royal python in this picture will often bite its victim before crushing it. Heat sensors on the snake's nose help it find its warm-blooded prey.

### PHYSICAL CHARACTERISTICS
Pythons are the world's longest snakes. Some species grow to a length of 30 feet.

### HABITAT
Most pythons and boas live in tropical places, in or near the water. The royal python spends the daylight hours basking in the sun or resting in a tree, cave, or burrow. Like many reptiles, the python hunts at night.

### PREY
When the sun goes down the snake stalks its prey or lies in wait at a water hole. It smells for food by flicking its tongue. The python likes to eat birds and mammals, such as deer, wild boar, and mice. Imagine how many mice it would take to fill a 30-foot-long snake!

# Behind the Scenes

The scaly and slimy creatures in this book were photographed by David G. Burder. David lives in London, England, but he often travels around the world in search of strange and interesting animals to photograph in 3-D.

Pictures made with regular cameras look flat. David uses 3-D photography because it creates depth. He built four different 3-D cameras especially for this project. Now, that is dedication!

Snapping pictures is only half the job of the 3-D photographer. After he lays down his cameras, David goes into his darkroom and makes the type of magical 3-D prints you see in this book—and in all The Nature Company 3-D books.

You might think that capturing these animals on film was a bit scary. How would you like to be face to face with a boa constrictor or a scorpion? For David it is all in a day's work—and part of a job which he finds challenging and rewarding.